ABSTRACT

This paper describes techniques which take advantage
of word arrangement to make possible large, high-speed
magnetic-core memories. Economy is obtained by means of a
two-coordinate system using diffused junction rectifiers as
steering diodes. By taking advantage of the recovery time
of these rectifiers, automatic rewrite selection is obtained
in a similar sense to that provided by a biased switch core.
The functions of sense and inhibit are combined on one winding contributing towards the reduction of the familiar four-
wire to a two-wire configuration. Finally, the customary
core array geometry is rearranged to facilitate winding each
of the two remaining wires as a balanced twisted-pair transmission line to eliminate the post-write disturb signal on
the now combined sense/inhibit line.

TABLE OF CONTENTS

DIODE-STEERED LINEAR MAGNETIC-CORE MEMORY

1. Introduction

The purpose of this paper is to present some original
techniques for surmounting well-known shortcomings in the
familiar coincident-current random access memory using
ferromagnetic cores as storage elements. These techniques
are intended for use as an extension to the more recently
favored word-arranged memory configuration, and the two
combined will yield higher speeds at lower costs for large
arrays than will either the coincident-current, or the
conventional word-arranged configuration. An illustrative
model containing transistorized peripheral equipment has
been constructed and tested. Using low-drive cores,
(coercive force less than 0.6 ampere-turn) the model exhibits
an access time of one microsecond and a cycle time of four.

2. History

The problems arising out of the application of conventional coincident-current selection to a large memory array
(say, 10,000 words) can be summarized easily. Assuming the
use of high-drive cores to store a word 60 bits long, the
drive requirements approximate 600 milliamperes at 45 volts.
The noise level (sum of the "disturbed zero and one" signals)

- 4 -

in such an array (100 x 100 x 60) requires special measures
be taken to successfully extract the information content on
the sense windings from the total signal. One such measure
is strobing, made possible because the peak of the undesired
signal, though large, does not coincide with the peak of the
desired one. With a large number of memory planes, this
method becomes increasingly difficult to instrument, as the
strobing time no longer remains the same for each plane, but
must be synchronized with both the transmission time between
planes, and the peaking time tolerance of the cores.

A second possible solution is to integrate [1] the signal
over two cycles so as to effect a cancellation of the undesired
signal component by cycling the contributing cores through a
complete hysteresis loop, $(\Delta \phi = 0)$ but this technique is
deleterious to high-speed operation and demanding of equipment as well.

A potential solution is provided by the so-called
word-arranged, or linear memory proposed by the National
Bureau of Standards [2]. This arrangement delegates to the
memory cores only the role of storage. Selection of the
desired word must be accomplished otherwise. This poses the
possibility of applying full drive power to the cores of the
selected word, and zero drive power to the remaining cores
in the memory. The discrimination problem is thereby
reduced to one of distinguishing between the output levels

- 5 -

of an "undisturbed one" signal and a "disturbed zero." Since
these are in the ratio of greater than six to one, this is
easily done ... but at the price of a driver per word.

A compromise solution is the use of a biased switch core
for each word of the memory. Since the switch core may be
selected by two-way coincident-current drive, this reduces
the number of drivers needed, in a square N-word array, from
N to $2\sqrt{N}$. Though metallic switch cores have better
saturation characteristics (resulting in smaller outputs from
partial excitation) than do ferromagnetic cores, the penalty
of this arrangement is that it results in $2(\sqrt{N}-1)$ half-
selected switch cores, so that the memory cores of $2(\sqrt{N}-1)$
words other than the selected one are subjected to some
disturbing drive power, again raising the specter of a
signal to noise problem. Additionally, the configuration
consisting of a switch core loaded by a line of memory cores
behaves like a very lossy, non-linear, and variable load.
The load current on the other hand must be relatively
independent of the number of cores in the "one" state. A
suggested [3] solution to this problem is to use two cores
per bit, so arranged that every pair contains one core in
each of the two possible states, thereby presenting a constant
load to the switch core. For a large array, this is very
costly. A better approach is needed.

3. Principle of Diode-Steered Linear Memory

Such an approach is the diode-steered system illustrated in Figure 1. The operation and advantages of this paper configuration are almost self-evident. Each core is threaded by three wires, a selection line, a sense line, and an inhibit line. A selection line threads all the cores of the same word, a sense and inhibit line (neither shown) thread all cores in the same bit position. A "read" is effected by turning on one X-read and one Y-read current switch, thereby supplying full drive current to the cores of only one word, and zero drive current to the remaining. This is followed by turning on the corresponding X- and Y-write current switches to "rewrite" the cores of the same word, using the signals on the sense windings to control the inhibit line drivers in such a way as not to "rewrite" cores previously in the "zero" state. A 10,000 word memory of this kind would require 20,000 diodes and 400 switches. The sense line noise problem is minimal, and relatively fast access is possible, since there is no theoretical limitation on the current for the "read" drive; the necessarily selective "rewrite" drive must hew approximately to the customary 2:1 selection ratio.

Practically, this system has a potentially serious weakness. The non-zero storage time of real diodes is here exacerbated by the open circuit into which the diode must

recover after conducting in the forward direction. During
access to the memory, an unrecovered diode presents a
spurious path to cores other than those of the selected word.
The consequences of this are twofold. The current switches
must supply additional power which will, in turn, manifest
itself as noise on the sense windings. This effect is
multiplied by the number of diodes in an unrecovered state.

However, realization that every "read" will be followed
by a "rewrite," and every "erase" by a "write" raises the
possibility of using this very characteristic of slow
recovery to tag that word in the memory which has been
subjected to the first, but not the second, of the basic
two cycle regimen. If the magnitude of the "write/rewrite"
current pulse should coinicde with the value necessary to
sweep out the injected carriers and restore the diode to its
initial state, several very attractive features would obtain;'
namely, elimination of half the number of required diodes,
automatic rewrite selection in the same sense as may be
obtained by the use of biased switch cores [1], effective
realization of the proposed approach, and a starting point
in the solution of the problem of obtaining large and high-
speed economical core memories.

The existence of diodes with characteristics which
match the current switching range of available magnetic
core materials, 0.3 to 0.6 ampere-turns, and 0.3 to 2.0

microseconds, is readily established.

Though diode manufacturers do not customarily publish the somewhat unusual data required here, investigation shows that junction diodes when biased with a relatively large value of current in the forward direction will conduct a considerable transient flow in the reverse direction if subjected immediately to a voltage source of reversed polarity. This transient current is characterized by a very fast rise to some peak value followed by a somewhat slower decay to zero. The peak value may be considerably greater than the amplitude of the bias current. However, if circuit-limited to some lesser maximum, the transient rises rapidly to the limiting value, holds steady, and finally decays to zero. An explanation of this phenomenon lies in the great number of minority carriers injected into the base of the diode by the bias current, and subsequently swept out by the reverse voltage pulse. More specifically, for any arbitrarily large amplitude of bias current, I_f, (limited by allowable temperature rise) the time of conduction, T_r, of the subsequent transient, I_r, is equal to T_d, (a function of I_f) and essentially independent of the time of conduction, T_f, of the bias current for $T_f > T_d$. However, for $T_f < T_d$, I_r may be circuit-limited to some value kI_f such that, for a wide range of I_f and T_f, $T_r = T_f$. Germanium junction diodes have been found which

- 9 -

lend themselves to use with values of k varying between
1/3 and 2/3 . The principal determinants seem to be the
material and the base thickness.

For the magnetic cores employed in our experiments,
RCA 222M2, the diode IN92 is well suited. Biased with a
forward current of 400 milliamperes for 1.5 microseconds,
(the turnover time for RCA 222M2 cores at 400 milliamperes
drive) and circuit-limited in the reverse direction to 200
milliamperes, the IN92 supports transient conduction at
this amplitude for 1.5 microseconds before turning off;
i.e., assuming a very high value of resistance in the reverse
direction. See Figure 2.

The half-drive reverse value of 200 milliamperes permits
rewrite control to be effected through a second 200 milli-
ampere winding. This aiding coincidence is quite contrary
to the inhibit coincidence of conventional coincident-current
memories, and were this aiding current to be supplied by means
of a third winding, the induced voltage would be of opposite
polarity to that on a parallel sense winding registering a
"one" output. Since it is relatively easy to prevent a
voltage of such polarity from saturating the sense amplifier
at the end of the sense line, it seems possible to use a
single winding to perform the functions both of "sense" and
"rewrite," and thereby reduce the number of windings from
three to two.

4. Construction of the Model

To corroborate these ideas, a four word model memory was fabricated having two pair each of X- and Y-selector lines. A block diagram is shown in Figure 3. The cores are RCA type 222M2 (300 to 450 milliamperes for full drive); the diodes are type IN92; the current switches in the X-lines are Raytheon transistors, type 2N426, in the Y-lines, Sylvania or RCA type 2N385. Two transistors in parallel are used for each current switch to avoid overdissipation for high repetition rates during testing. Low-drive cores are used for the same reason.

Each steering diode is normally back-biased by 30 volts. When, after conduction, it presents a low resistance to back-voltage, the transient current is circuit-limited to a maximum of 200 milliamperes. To select word W_{11} , lines W_{01} and W_{10} are alerted, providing a current source from minus three volts on selection line X_1 , and a constant current sink of 550 milliamperes to minus fifteen volts on selector line Y_1 . The six volt supply delivers about 150 milliamperes, the minus 24 volt supply acts as a sink for about 400 milliamperes. The X-line current source supplies about 800 milliamperes with about 400 being conducted through the memory selector line. After lines W_{01} and W_{10} are released, automatic rewrite takes place with the rewrite driver supplying the additional current necessary.

- 11 -

5. Experimental Results

Additional circuitry to that indicated in Figure 3 is used to continually "read" and "rewrite" one core of one word in the model memory while the total number of cores in the "one" state of that word (60 cores) is varied by means of a bias winding control. Measurements show that the current on the memory selector line varies only between 400 and 420 milliamperes as the size of the memory load (number of cores in the "one" state) is varied between zero and sixty. This attests to the constant current nature of the drive.

The maximum "disturbed-zero" signal per core under this current regime is ten millivolts. Since there are no partially excited cores in this system, a signal level greater than this on the sense line foretells a "one" output (100 millivolts). The circuitry is adjusted so that a signal level of 60 milli-volts at the input to the sense amplifier turns on the rewrite driver in coincidence with a read-alert signal. With the cores used here, this takes place 0.9 microseconds after the selector-line drivers are turned on. See Figure 4. The rewrite driver remains on for two microseconds to insure that the core is completely "rewritten," and carries the cycle time to about three microseconds. After a delay of another microsecond while the post-write disturb signal on the combined sense/rewrite line settles, the memory is again ready for access.

6. Discussion

These experimental results should not be considered definitive, but rather illustrative. The time necessary for the "read" portion of a cycle can be much reduced over that indicated here by the application of overdrive current to high-drive cores. Further, access may be accomplished well in advance of the total switching time of the core-type used. As previously indicated, it is not necessary to fully reset one-state cores before "rewriting" them. Of course, caution must be exercised in the case of an erase/write cycle to ensure at least partial reseting of each core in the word. This may take somewhat longer than a read/rewrite cycle.

The use of overdrive current will require steering diodes with matching characteristics; though the amplitude of the read-drive current is limited only by practical considerations of power capacity and temperature rise, the portion of the rewrite-drive current contributed by the diode is limited, for any single core-type, to a value which will not compromise the approximate criterion of a 2:1 current selection ratio. This implies a diode with a value of $k < 1/2$, (as well as the requisite bias current capacity) and was satisfied in the experimental model described here by replacing the 1N92 with a diode having a thinner base, the 1N91.

As may be seen in Figure 4, a significant contribution

to the total cycle time is the one microsecond post-write disturb signal on the combined sense/rewrite line. It is the result of sending partial rewrite current down a long line threading a large number of cores (one for each word) and then quickly replacing the low output impedance of the source by its high cut-off output impedance. Since this circuit action is irremediable, the solution lies in not charging the line.

The impedance presented by the line to the rewrite driver is that of the incremental permeability (virtually identical in the "disturbed-zero" and "disturbed-one" states for square-loop material) of all but one of the cores, plus the switching load of the remaining one, i.e., a sequence of lumped inductors distributed along the length of the line. If a wire located adjacent to the sense/rewrite line is substituted for the ground plane, this long line may be converted into a two-wire transmission line and terminated in a resistor. If, in addition, the second wire is twisted about the first and threaded through the cores as well, the partial rewrite current required of the rewrite driver is reduced by one-half, and the twisted pair transmission line is virtually impervious to stray magnetic fields. The value of the terminating resistor may be determined experimentally to be that which has the greatest effect in reducing the duration of the post-write disturb voltage.

- 14 -

Using several of the different core-types available, 4000-core lines have been assembled having acceptable transmission times (100 millimicroseconds $\pm$ 50%). These could all be terminated with a value of resistance varying between 200 and 400 ohms, so as to obtain the effect shown in Figure 6. Though the terminating value determined experimentally was found to be not very critical, this value always compared favorably (within 50%) with a calculated value based upon the incremental permeability of the core and the measured capacitance of the twisted pair transmission line.

The selector line may escape this treatment since it is but one or two core words in length (say, about 120 cores). Of course, the advantage of having to supply only one-half switching current with a threaded twisted pair is independent of the termination, and any second loop or turn can accomplish the same effect.

In practice, these transmission line arrays can be fabricated by drilling out a phenolic (or other) board of a thickness equal to the core height, with 50, or 80 mill holes, on 100 mill centers, filling the holes with cores, sealing them temporarily in place with a layer of cellophane (or other transluscent tissue) on each face, and wiring the assembly as shown in Figure 5. A board so wired will contain some number of word selector lines and digit lines, the latter being connected by digit position to the corresponding

- 15 -

lines in the subsequent plane, so that finally, all the
identical digit lines are connected in long twisted pair
transmission lines. This assembly technique serves to fix
the geometry of the array, and consequently its distributed
capacity. In order to strike a balance between the "characteristic impedance" and the transmission time of the line,
the distributed capacity may be varied by varying the hole
spacing.

7. Conclusions

Using these techniques with "high-speed" cores, it should
be possible to build large memories at attractive costs with a
cycle time of two, and an access time of 0.7 microseconds.
Current researches into impulse, and partial switching may
reduce these times even further, although not without some
increase in cost. The upper boundary for speed in this system
is determined by the transmission time delay on the combined
sense/rewrite line, and although this may be reduced by short-
ening the length of the line, such action would cause serious
inroads into the economies effected by means of the large array.

As remarked previously, the memory selector lines are of
relatively short length, so that it would not deleteriously
effect the system operation to increase this length by a
factor of two or three; i.e., to string along a memory selector
line the cores of two or three words rather than only one. In
this way, with only little more peripheral equipment, a

simultaneous two- or three-word readout per access could be accomplished providing the possibility of some degree of computer advance control. The value of this feature is being currently underscored by the continuing imbalance in operating speed between arithmetic and the fastest available memory units.

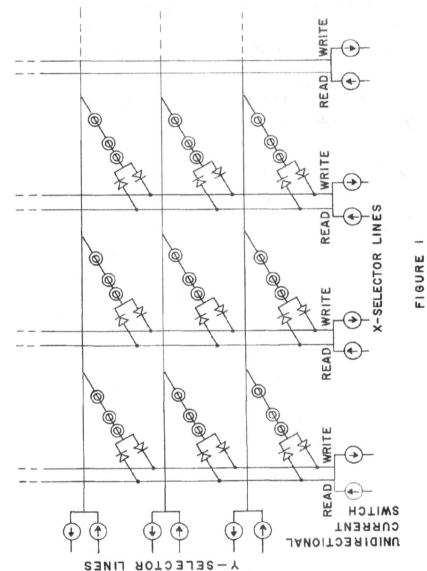

FIGURE 1

SCHEMATIC DRAWING OF DIODE-STEERED SELECTION SYSTEM FOR LINEAR
MEMORY ARRAY

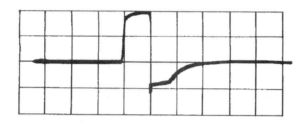

FIGURE 2

TRACING OF PHOTOGRAPH SHOWING VOLTAGE WAVE-
FORM ACROSS ONE OHM RESISTOR IN SERIES
WITH STEERING DIODE, TYPE IN92 ; VERTICAL
SCALE, 200 MILLIVOLTS/ DIVISION ; HORIZONTAL
SCALE, ONE MICROSECOND/ DIVISION

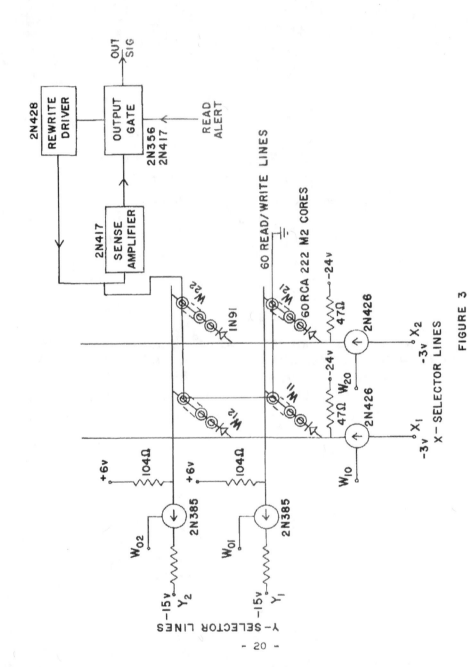

FIGURE 3

BLOCK DIAGRAM OF FOUR—WORD MODEL MEMORY

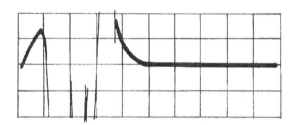

FIGURE 4

TRACING OF PHOTOGRAPH SHOWING VOLTAGE WAVE-
FORM AT INPUT TO SENSE AMPLIFIER; VERTICAL
SCALE, 50 MILLIVOLTS/DIVISION; HORIZONTAL
SCALE, ONE MICROSECOND/DIVISION

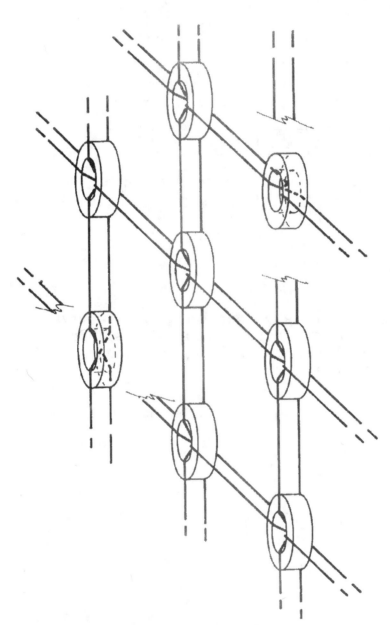

FIGURE 5

CORE ARRAY WIRING

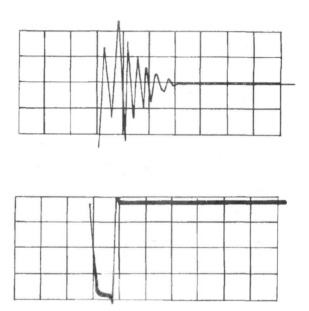

FIGURE 6

TRACING OF PHOTOGRAPH SHOWING VOLTAGE
WAVEFORM AT OUTPUT OF REWRITE DRIVER CONNECTED
TO 2000 CORE LINE SHORT-CIRCUITED, AND CORRECTLY
TERMINATED; VERTICAL SCALE, FIVE VOLTS/DIVISION;
HORIZONTAL SCALE, ONE MICROSECOND/DIVISION

Bibliography

[1]   J. Rajchman, "A Myriabit Magnetic-Core Matrix Memory,"
      Proc. I.R.E., Vol. 41, October 1953.

[2]   National Bureau of Standards, "Progress on Computer
      Components," October 1954-March 1955.

[3]   University of Illinois Digital Computer Laboratory,
      "Report No. 80, On the Design of a Very High Speed
      Computer," October 1957.